This book is dedicated to the people of the world by the Children of the Tsunami.

Published in Thailand by:
Sirivatana Interprint Public Co., Ltd.
76/76 Charoenkrung 57
Sathorn
Bangkok 10120

 ISBN 974-93631-1-6

# Children of the Tsunami

## Khao Lak - A Story of Hope

Compiled by the Students of Bangkok Patana School

Edited by Robin Nagy

*Bangkok Patana Students and Pak Weep School children.* © Nicholas Mak

**Children of the Tsunami**
*Khao Lak – A Story of Hope*

# FOREWORD

*"Give a man a fish and you feed him for a day. Teach him how to fish and you feed him for a lifetime."*

These enigmatic words originate from Lao Tzu, the founder of Taoism. In creating this book we hope to make a difference for the long-term, not just superficially. This book is a home-grown project in which students at Bangkok Patana School have helped children of the Tsunami affected region of Khao Lak, Thailand to tell their own stories and to help themselves by raising money for their own education and that of the region.

The Asian Tsunami of December 26th 2004 was one of the most devastating natural disasters of modern times. It affected millions of people over a vast area of the globe and its impact will no doubt be felt for many years to come. In turn, the Tsunami spawned one of the biggest aid operations the world has ever seen and millions of dollars were donated by countries, organisations and individuals all over the world.

Located in the capital city of Thailand, over 500km away from the Tsunami affected area of Khao Lak and Phuket, Bangkok Patana School is one of the biggest international schools in the region. On 26th December, we too felt the impact of the Tsunami, and many of our staff, students and extended community returned with their own incredible stories of survival against the odds from their holidays in Southern Thailand, Sri Lanka and the Maldives. We also lost members of our community, notably in Khao Lak, Thailand where several of our students died. It seemed appropriate therefore, for us to look for a project in the Khao Lak region in which to involve ourselves as a small part of the overall relief effort which was already well underway. It was apparent that people around the world wanted to know what was going on in the Tsunami affected countries. They wanted to see where their donations had gone and whether their generosity had made a real difference to people's lives.

In June 2005, a group of 24 of students from Bangkok Patana School visited four local schools in Khao Lak, which had been affected by the Tsunami: Pak Weep, Bang Niang, Bang Sak and Watkommaneeyakhet School.

Our project would involve the students of Bangkok Patana School collecting artwork, stories and photographs from the children of Khao Lak to help them create a book of their own which would tell their story to a world who had already shown so much interest in helping them. Our book project mission was simple: children would be helping children to help themselves. The end result would be a message of thanks to the world at large from the children of Khao Lak. More importantly, the project would provide a means by which these children could make money to pay for their own education and the rebuilding and resourcing of the schools of the Tsunami affected region.

The visit by students of Bangkok Patana School took place at the end of June and beginning of July 2005 and we spent five busy days collecting material for the book as well as carrying out other projects in and around Khao Lak and conducting language and craft activities with the children. The main narrative in this book is based on the written accounts of the Students of Bangkok Patana School who went on the trip to Khao Lak. Everybody who has been a part of this project has been affected in some way by the experience. In the words of reflection of one of the students from Bangkok Patana School: "I came on this trip expecting to help others but instead I received the help. I learnt that every moment of your life matters; it shapes who you are in the future. I will try to treasure every moment not only of my life but in the lives of others. Through this project I learnt to appreciate everything and everyone and to always smile because it's priceless."

On our return to school in September 2005, a total of 52 students from Bangkok Patana School, now in Year 12, undertook the task of compiling the book from the material we had brought back in July. Therefore, including the children of Khao Lak who created all the artwork, this book represents the end result of the efforts of over a hundred highly motivated and creative children from both Thai and International backgrounds.

Khao Lak is an area of outstanding natural beauty, whose economy is heavily reliant on tourism. This book seeks to uncover the positive and to highlight stories of hope following the well documented tragic events of 26th December 2004. Khao Lak is well and truly open for business again and we hope that this book will play a part in encouraging tourists back to this beautiful region of Thailand which now needs the tourist dollar like never before.

Thank you for buying a copy of this book. All the profits will be used in directly benefiting the education of the children of the Tsunami affected region of Thailand. You can play an even bigger part in the recovery of the region by planning a visit to the beautiful beaches and islands of Thailand's Andaman coast.

Robin Nagy
Head of Year 12 and Tsunami Book Coordinator
Bangkok Patana School
October 2005

*Khao Lak Beach. © Nicholas Mak*

The Tsunami hitting Khao Lak. Note that the sea has completely drained out of Khao Lak bay in the photograph below:

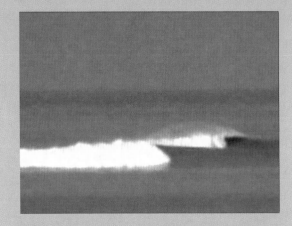

The time between the photograph on the bottom left and the one on the right is a matter of two minutes.

"On that day I went down to the beach with my friend. I looked at the sea and the tide had gone out a long way. I had a strange feeling that something was wrong. My friend didn't care and ran into the water. I watched the water rise up and up. I haven't seen my friend since that day."

When I was very young, maybe about seven years old, I remember my father reading a newspaper article about a tsunami hitting the coast of Japan. I remember asking: "...what's a tsunami, Dad?" My father interrupted his reading, looked up at me and said: "It's a wave in the sea so big that it can come ashore, smash buildings to pieces, wash away roads and kill many people." "Do we get Tsunamis here, Dad?" I lived in Scotland at the time and the largest waves I'd ever seen stayed firmly where they should be – in the sea. I just didn't understand the concept of a wave moving from where it should be (the sea) to where it most definitely shouldn't (the land). My father smiled at me: "No, of course we don't," he said. "But, if we did, would it kill me?" I don't recall my father's exact words in response but I understood that as tsunamis were so rare, it was extremely unlikely that I would encounter one; if I did, I probably wouldn't survive.

It's ironic that bad things can bring out the best in people. And it was our shared humanity that brought us, a group of students and staff from my school, Bangkok Patana, to the devastated communities and rubble strewn beaches of Khao Lak, Thailand, six months later.

*Willem from Bangkok Patana School with the children of Khao Lak.*
*© Nicholas Mak*

"I am Prapa - a young girl who experienced the devastation of the events of December 26th 2004. I was playing on the water front when the waves came in and though my mother could warn me, she couldn't reach my sister. My sister will never reach twenty one as she perished in the waves. We mourn the loss of my sister. After the Tsunami, I feel inspired to become a doctor, to help people in need."

Prapasri presenting her artwork for the camera. © Robin Nagy

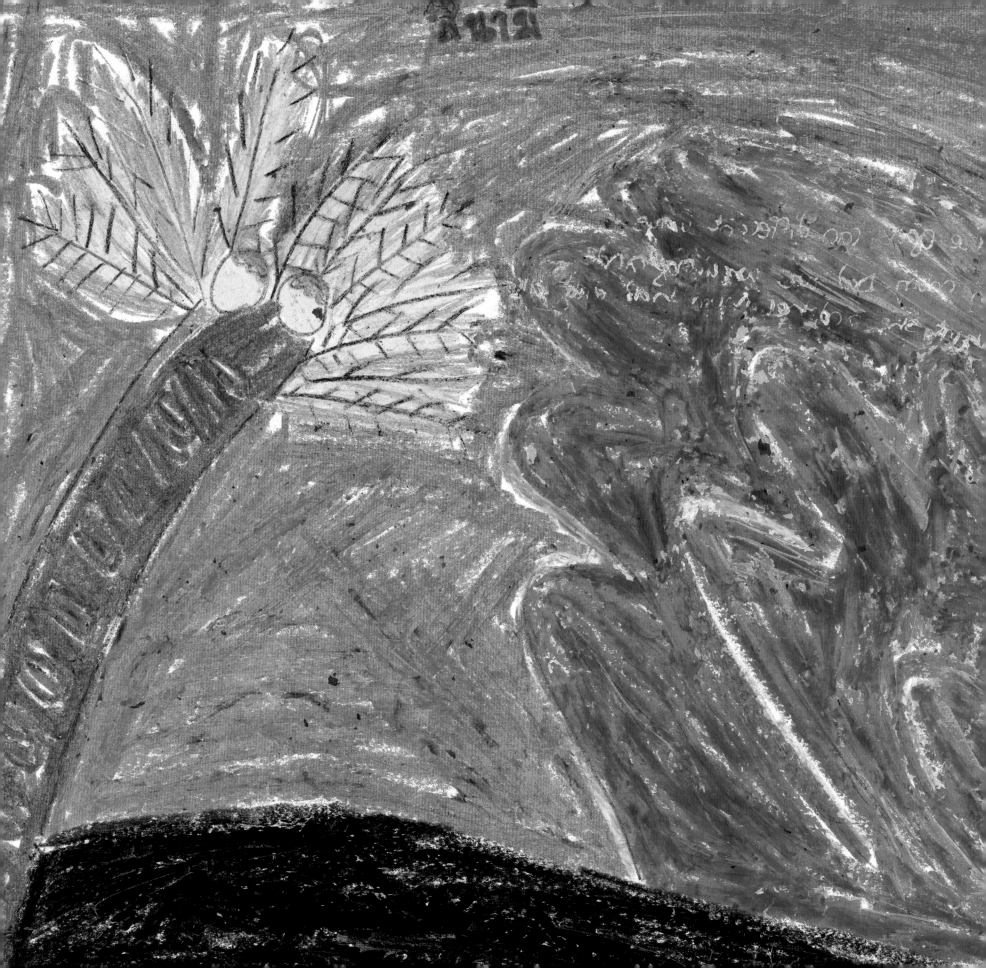

*Tsunami hitting the beach, by Wilasinee.*

"My name is Wilasinee; my nickname is May. I am in Year 3 and I hope that everyone is happy and safe. Although I was affected by the wave, I will try to move on and put it into the past. My house is gone. When the Tsunami struck, my whole family was separated as we all ran in different directions. My Father thought that my Mother and I were killed. Although we no longer have a house, we still have each other."

*Photo: © Nicholas Mak*

**F**rom Bangkok, we flew down to Phuket and then drove out of our privileged 'urban world', where money is the answer to all ills, to Khao Lak where a different set of values prevails. Admittedly, money helps, it helps an awful lot, in fact there was a lot of money in Khao Lak before the Tsunami, but what I saw there now was damage beyond the remedy of just coloured pieces of paper with assigned monetary values.

When arriving in Phuket Airport, a bit further south of our destination, I was unsure of what feelings I would encounter and what my own feelings and emotions would be. Would there still be a large amount of devastation or would the members of the Khao Lak community have already moved on? I wondered how the beach paradise, which I had visited just 10 months before, would have changed.

I remember thinking that our combined 'spending money' for the trip would probably have provided a month's worth of food for the people living in the tents and wooden shelters dotted along the higher ground, overlooking smashed hotels and resorts these people once might have worked in or even owned - talk about a guilt trip!

"As a result of the terrible Tsunami, there are many people and organisations conducting activities and donating clothes and stationery. Even the number of teachers in my school has increased from 4 to 6 now. I am very grateful to all those people who have come down here to do various activities and to play with us. They have helped us to put the Tsunami behind us. Sharing knowledge and giving support has allowed people with no jobs to get jobs and earn money that will help them return to their normal lives. I think that the Tsunami has made us all humbler and lessened the difference between the rich and the poor."

Photo: © Robin Nagy

*A tsunami scene on display at Bang Niang School.*

We all came so 'prepared', *Samsonite* luggage, designer clothes and (of course) mobile phones. We soon learned that these items weren't going to help us very much on this trip.

There is little or no preparation when it comes to dealing with death. It seems trivial to mention that just before the trip, my dog died. He was seven years old and I couldn't help thinking about him. You might consider the death of a pet as inconsequential and I suppose it is, but at the time words couldn't express how empty I felt at his loss.

To bed and the all too sudden wake-up at 7am (this was new to a lot of us, who ritually slept away the mornings during summer holidays). Following breakfast, we made our way to Pak Weep School passing the devastated landscape which incorporated a marooned police boat – number 813. The boat was sitting high and dry, stranded on a hill several hundred meters inland and had been made famous overnight by worldwide TV coverage of the Tsunami.

*Left :   The marooned police boat – number 813 serves as a memorial to the Tsunami. © Robin Nagy*

*Right :  Girls from Pak Weep School. © Nicholas Mak*

"It was the 26th of December and I was following my Mum through the department store in Phuket. I heard someone shout "the water is running away" and I thought, "that's impossible". My Dad then came and picked us up and we drove into the mountains. Two days later, we set off back home, but all the time we were worried that the wave was coming back. Five days later we received news that it was safe to return, so together we drove home."

*A boy drawing at*
*Watkommaneeyakhet School.*
© Robin Nagy

"My nickname is Pai, my first name is Machaphorn. My parents used to work on the 'Nang Tong Sorng' shore. My Dad was a construction worker and my Mum worked in a laundry. I will never forget Sunday, 26th December 2004. Both my Mum and Dad left for work as usual, but my Dad never returned. We finally collected his body from the government officials on the 18th April. Things looked very bleak for what seemed like a very long time. At last my Mum has managed to find some temporary work in a school. We are slowly moving forward."

*School boy lining up at Bang Sak School.*
*© Robin Nagy*

*Temporary housing at Pak Weep Shelter. © Robin Nagy*

One of the most pressing issues in Khao Lak is finding affordable but good quality, permanent housing for the displaced population, who have been living in sheltered accommodation or tents for several months now. When we visited in July, the occupants of the Pak Weep Shelter were looking forward to moving from their plywood room to a purpose built house in one of the new estates which are springing up around the Khao Lak region. One such new housing estate is the King of Thailand's Project.

As we drove along, the awesome force of the Tsunami became more and more apparent – this was not a game. The mood changed from the excitement, usual at the beginning of a school trip, to one of apprehension and reflection. To see the destruction, the washed out buildings, the fallen trees, the piles of rubbish, was eye-opening. But then to also see the beauty of Khao Lak, the breathtaking greenery, the beautiful mountains, the pristine water of the Andaman Sea, just showed me that all was not lost. As we arrived at Pak Weep School my anxiety rose: just how do you comfort a child orphaned so suddenly? How should you behave around people who have lost everything? Within minutes none of our lives would be the same again.

*Houses on the new estate at the King of Thailand's Project.* © Robin Nagy

*Pak Weep School welcomes Bangkok Patana, Khao Lak June 2005. © Nicholas Mak*

As we entered the school grounds we were greeted by the most amazing sight; a sea of smiling children waving roses and a 'Welcome Bangkok Patana School' sign. In a split second our apprehension and anxiety evaporated.

One of our group later commented: "When we arrived my mind wandered back to a time when I was in a similar situation to them, when I had lost the one person that mattered the most in my life – my father. Even though I was trying so hard to push the tears away, to show the kids a happy side of me, it was hard. I felt tears start to sting my eyes and trickle down my cheeks. I knew that I had to hold my tears back and show these kids a happy exterior which may just help to signal the possibility of moving on."

*Pak Weep boy makes a funny face for the camera. © Robin Nagy*

We got off the bus and all gathered in a group in front of the main school building. The whole of Pak Weep School was also gathered. The thirty girls holding the roses were lined up opposite us; with shy smiles they handed us the roses and then joined their hands together (as if in prayer) to give the traditional 'Wai' of greeting and respect, characteristically Thai.

All the children were beaming with smiles; they were acting as if nothing had happened. I don't know what we were expecting, children with haunted looks perhaps, children looking miserable, sad, even angry, I don't know what, but not this. We began to really admire these kids, to respect them and their apparent ability to draw a line under the horror of what had just happened to them and to move on.

Photo: © Nicholas Mak

"My name is Beer, I am 11 years old and that day was my birthday. I was very happy as my Mum was taking me to the beach as a treat. However, at around 10 am, I heard people screaming, "run away, a giant wave is heading towards us!" I was very scared, but on hearing the warnings, my mother and I ran up the nearby mountain, until the wave had retreated. Once we felt safe, we came back down the mountain and took shelter in a neighbour's house, as ours had completely disappeared. My Dad had left for the beach before us and never came back. His body was later found on the shore. This left my mother and me in shock and total despair, but it has made me realise the importance of fulfilling our dreams. I would like to become a teacher when I grow up. I understand that little children are our future generation and as a teacher, I can try and give them the best opportunities I can."

*The aftermath of the Tsunami saw many dead bodies floating in the ocean, as seen by Ta.*

" My name is Ta and I am lucky to live at home with my parents and my sister, but I miss my grandfather who was caught in the Tsunami. I also miss my friends from school, who I haven't seen since the wave came. I am happy to see the volunteers and visitors though, as they are all good people, helping us become less lonely."

Photo: © Nicholas Mak

*Girl at Watkommaneeyakhet School playing with a paper helicopter.* © *Robin Nagy*

*"In my opinion, the Tsunami has taught us humility and we have realised mistakes that we have made. Life is too short to make wrong decisions, to insult and bully. The Tsunami has taught us not to take chances, but to make the most of them."*

*"My name is Nawee. On Sunday, I was planning to take my friends to the beach, but the Tsunami came so I ran up the mountain. There were so many people fleeing from the Tsunami up there."*

*Drawing by Nawee.*

We had a short assembly where Mr. Nagy, our teacher and trip coordinator, told the whole school the main reason we were here, '...to collect your stories and pictures for a book...'

We made our introduction first in English then in Thai. Most of us felt a little shy having to shout out our names.

We began our visit with some 'ice-breaker' activities which usually means you have to make a complete fool of yourself in front of everyone. Beforehand we thought that the kids would be the ones who would have to lighten up and would be in need of 'ice breaking' - lesson number one (the first of many): it was the other way around. The children took us into their lives in an instant and never let go.

*Nick from Bangkok Patana School finds it hard to let go. © Nicholas Mak*

น้อง แอง

ด.ญ กุดารัตน์     ทองแท้

*Sudarat's drawing shows the beauty of Khao Lak.*

*New Born. New Hope. New Life.*
*Safe in the hands of his Grandma.*
*© Nicholas Mak*

On December 27, 2004, the day after the Tsunami struck and changed the lives of hundreds of thousands of people, hope in the form of a newborn child inspired the local people of Khao Lak. The baby's mother had miraculously survived the vicious torrent of seawater by hanging on to the side of a building, fearing for her life as well as that of her unborn child.

When a group from Bangkok Patana School first visited the temporary shelter near Pak Weep School on January 29, 2005, the community excitedly brought us to see this infant and shared with us the tale of his dramatic entry into this world. It was clear that this baby brought hope to the local people whose homes had been destroyed.

This baby had become a symbol of hope in the community and was held in the highest regard, but her mother did not make a fuss. Her gratitude at having survived needed no words. This story shows that hope is abundant amongst the people of Khao Lak in the aftermath of the Tsunami.

*A destroyed resort at Khao Lak.* © Robin Nagy

**Children of the Tsunami**
*Khao Lak – A Story of Hope*

"It was a Sunday on the 26th of December, so school was closed that day. I was at home watching TV with my sister Toey. When it started switching on and off, I thought that it was an electrical fault, so I turned it off and went to buy some snacks with my grandma. Just as we left the house, we noticed that the numerous bamboo trees that grew by the beach were moving and shaking. I shrugged it off, thinking the workers were cutting down trees. Just as we were about to leave, I noticed a large wave in the distance. This prompted my grandma to hurry my younger sister and her friends out of the stream, where they were playing. She brought us up to the mountain and we sought refuge there for many days. I wasn't able to go to school until my Daddy said it was alright again. After a period of time, we came down from the mountain and returned to our homes once again. Thank you Grandma."

Photo: © Robin Nagy

Drawing by Jiwanan.

"My name is Chutikarn, but family and friends call me Fang for short. When it happened I was watching TV and the lights started to flicker. For safety, I turned off the TV. My sister, Guang, said that the bed was wiggling. Then suddenly, many cars drove by and they said that the waves were coming. Dad came in and said, "Quick, quick! Get in the car!" I was really scared. Dad drove us up to the mountains and Mum told me not to cry, so I stopped. I saw the giant waves and Mum told me that it was a tsunami. In the morning, Dad took me home and then suddenly many cars drove by and said that the waves were coming again. My house floor wiggled and I was very scared. I am happy that it won't happen again."

One of our party, I think, speaks for all or us: "Five minutes into activities however, my general conclusion was that kids were cute to look at but not so cute to try and instruct. After fruitlessly trying to explain that these bits of paper were flowers, f-l-o-w-e-r-s, 'dok mai' - look! - you plant them in the ground, how pretty! – I quickly learned that for the kids to understand what they were to do, it was necessary for me to forget who I was and temporarily be one of them. Yet to stand in front of a group of watchful eyes and bawl out "head, shoulders, knees and toes" when I knew perfectly well where my body parts belonged, was honestly mortifying."

As the activities continued, we became less and less inhibited and I knew the 'ice' had well and truly been broken not by us but by the kids. Soon enough, the whole group was involved and it made me smile to see my usually boisterous friends sitting with a child or two on their lap making funny noises to entertain them.

I'm not sure who enjoyed the activities most - the kids or us.

*Ice-breaker activities with Pak Weep pupils. © Robin Nagy*

We reassembled and our group was then split up into smaller groups in order to visit different classrooms. We had brought with us gift boxes made by the Elementary Division of Bangkok Patana School. Each class from our school had been given the task of making and filling gift boxes to be presented to specific boys or girls of the same age in Khao Lak. The idea was that our pupils would have a better idea of what someone of their own age might need or want. The boxes were a great success and were filled with all sorts of things from teddy bears to protractors.

As I sat there listening to the children speak about their loss; '....Mum, Dad, Uncle, Auntie, my friend, my brother, my sister, my neighbour, the lady that cooked noodles on the street...' it made my loss fade into a different level of grief.

*Girl receiving gift box at Pak Weep School.*
*© Nicholas Mak*

*Natasha's Story.*

ปัจจุบันชีวิตหนู
ตอนนี้มีพี่ๆอาสาสมัครมาให้กำลังใจ
และมีของมาแจกอีก พี่ๆทำมีกิจกรรมหลายๆอย่าง
มาให้หนูได้เล่น และได้ไปทำกิจกรรมที่อื่นๆ
อีกด้วย ตอนนี้หนูมีความสุขมากๆ
ถึงแม้ว่าจะสูญเสียใครไปก็ตาม
หนูชอบกรุงเทพที่ มาเชิกหุ่นเจ้าขุนทอง
และยังมีพี่ๆอาสาสมัครจากที่อื่นๆ

มาให้กำลังใจ

ด.ญ.นาตาชา หมานเจริญ ป.๔

"My name is Natasha. The volunteers here support us and even give us presents. They organise many different activities for us to play and take us on excursions. Right now, they have made me feel very happy, although I have lost people I cared for."

*All that is remaining of the original Bang Sak School is the flag pole. © Robin Nagy*

**B**ehind the smiles it was clear that the kids here had been traumatised. This trauma manifested itself in many different ways. For example, one little girl would only go to female members of the group. She held on to one of our party and cried bitterly if put down repeating the phrase 'pai mâe' ('go to Mummy' in Thai) over and over again. The whole community was traumatised, not just the children. This society was pulling together to move on from the devastation that left no one untouched. The children seemed to be a focus for the community, and yet nowhere was this spirit of quiet determination and hope more apparent than in the faces of the children themselves. These children taught us to be positive in everything we do. They taught me that when you lose a loved one, there is a time to mourn but after that is a time to re-build and to appreciate what you have left; to be glad to still have a house or a school to go to, that there is no sense in being sad all your life because you have lost someone important to you, because this will not bring them back.

We were also amazed at human resilience. The people here were literally rebuilding their lives. Houses were being built out of the rubble of destroyed buildings. The roads had been cleared and new schools and other community buildings were beginning to emerge. There was one school, Bang Sak, which was totally destroyed by the Tsunami. In fact the only thing which was left of the original school was a solitary flagpole in the middle of what had once been the playground, and yet, there it was - almost 'proud' to have survived the Tsunami with the students carrying on lessons in tents and temporary buildings up a nearby hill.

*Bang Sak School is being rebuilt on a new site. Clockwise from Top: Students gather in front of a temporary classroom; Robin Nagy holds up two (heavy) pupils in front of the new school buildings; Bangkok Patana students explain the book project idea. © Robin Nagy*

*Lessons in a temporary classroom.* © Robin Nagy

*Sawetree drew a happy scene of beautiful Khao Lak.*

เรื่อง แสนสวย

วันหนึ่งฉันไปทะเลกับเพื่อนแล้วเพื่อนของ
ฉันบอกว่าทะเลนี้สวยมากเลยแล้วเพื่อนฉัน
บอก ว่าไปเราไปเล่นน้ำ กันไปแล้วเพื่อนของ
ฉันบอกว่าทะเลนี้สวยมากเขาบอกว่าเราคอย
มาเที่ยวกันไหมมัยฉันบอกว่าพรุ่งนี้เรามา
เล่นมัยไม่ ฉันบอกว่าทะเลที่นี่มันเต้น แสนสวย
มากค่ะ

ด.ญ.สาวิตรี หาญทะ ป.5/1

*"My name is: Sawetree. One day I went to the sea with my friend. My friend told me that the sea was very beautiful today and she said, "Let's go play in the sea together." She asked me if I would come back again with her. She said that we should play again the next day because the sea is extremely beautiful."*

*Nawik's picture shows a boy running from the Tsunami.*

**Children of the Tsunami**
*Khao Lak – A Story of Hope*

The experience affected us all in many different ways. As another member of our group explained:

*"...Later that afternoon while I was slapping on some sun block lotion, worrying about sunburn, within a hundred meters of me were children who were missing a loved one. It made me think about how sad I get whenever a close friend of mine moves away to another country (all too common an occurrence on the International School scene). To me, even though keeping in touch is made possible by phone and the internet, it's still not the same as spending time together. But how trivial that all seemed when compared with what these kids were going through - major reality check!"*

*A view of Khao Lak beach. © Robin Nagy*

*The havoc caused by the floods of the Tsunami, by Taweephol.*

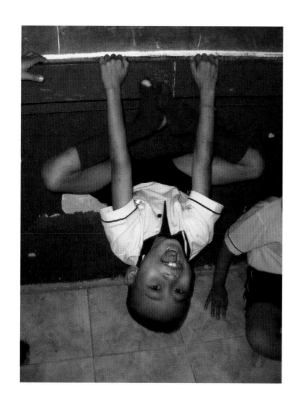

*Photos: © Macha Cauchois*

"On the 26th of December, the bright sun shone
I woke up early on a Sunday morning.
Just like Thai kids normally do
I sat in front of the TV.
My house turned into chaos,
I was scared but also curious.
The Tsunami rushed into me,
I quickly took my sister, together we ran as fast as we could
My Mum and Dad were running towards us.
Dad carried me with him
Mum and my sister were carried away by the water.
Dad made an impossible decision
What will we do now?
My Mum and sister are gone!
My heart is torn in two.
The house is no more.
I only have my Dad beside me now
And nothing else to hold."

*Montri's drawing from Bang Niang School.*

After visiting Pak Weep School, we walked to a nearby temporary shelter. It made me think about how we refer to the people living there as having had 'lost their homes' as if it were a careless act for which 'they' were partly responsible, a bit like leaving your umbrella on the bus. In reality the people here had left their homes only to return to find them, together with the furniture, clothes, photographs, money, car, food, blankets, bed and kitchen sink totally and utterly destroyed. But that's not all, the shops, the businesses, the jobs, the buses, the schools and the hospitals had also been demolished. But even here there was light at the end of the tunnel. Some of the children who had lost their homes were excited about moving into a brand new place which was even better than their old home. These new homes were being constructed as one of the King of Thailand's projects.

*A boy at the entrance to his temporary home in the Pak Weep Shelter.*
*© Robin Nagy*

*"My name is Kanyarat. My mother was at work when the Tsunami came and she hurried back to come and get me. We were going to pick up Grandma, but we couldn't because everyone said the big waves were coming. My Mum and I went up to the mountains and met our cousins who told us that my Dad was at work and had been hit by the big wave. I cried and was very sad. But by noon Daddy came back. I was so happy. We lived up on the mountain for several days and then we moved into the school playground."*

Photo: © Macha Cauchois

*Drawing of people clinging on to trees to escape waves by Kornkij.*

*Three Bang Sak boys with sock puppets © Robin Nagy*

"My name is Byoke and I am twelve years old. I was scared of the Tsunami as I had never seen anything like it before. I was also scared that so many people were dying. When I grow up I want to become a nurse, so that I can help people. My Mum and Dad have jobs again now."

*overleaf: Christian's vivid watercolour depicting
police boat number 813 in the Tsunami.*

"I am 13 years old and my name is Christian. I saw the Tsunami while I was fishing. I saw two
police boats and then saw the water go down and leave the boat on the beach. When the wave
came I didn't feel scared, I thought it was amazing. I'd never seen anything like that before, so
I didn't know that it was a tsunami. I saw some people running and I followed them. I climbed
up a coconut tree and the water came up to my waist. The second wave pushed me under the
water and I can't swim. I heard a foreign woman ask, "where's my son?" and saw another man
get buried in the sand. I have a scar on my leg from being under the water. My house is now gone.
We went up a mountain away from the beach and I was very thirsty, but no one had any water.
I felt sick. I went to a hospital, but I had to wait a very long time because there were so many
injured people.

Some of my friends are gone. I live with some people in the mountains and everything is alright.
I like to play the bass guitar and drums, but I lost them in the Tsunami. I bought a cheap guitar
because I wanted to carry on playing and sometimes there isn't much else to do. My house is
being built again and I want to live there with my dog Santa. My brother lives in Bangkok and
works for a fashion magazine.

When I'm older I want to sell boats. My mother's boat is under the water and her other one is used
for scuba diving."

Picture by Wiparat.

"My name is Nuntanut. The day of the disaster was the day that I went to Nam Klong with my aunt and sister. My aunt told us that the giant waves were coming and we should get into the car. We went to Pang Chang and were safe there, but I felt frightened as the earth shook. We stayed there for 3 days until we could go home again. I went to the beach and I saw lots of things scattered all over the ground. It was really scary when the earth shook."

No home, no possessions, but some things are more important than material wealth. A grandmother clings to the most important thing in her life. © Nicholas Mak

Jatuporn's drawing of the 813 police boat.

*Creating artwork for the book at
Watkommaneeyakhet School.
© Robin Nagy*

"My name is Witrack and I am 10 years old. On 26th of December I was asleep at home when my Mum woke me up and told me the wave was coming. We fled to the mountains and stayed there for one night. We found some food and later discovered that my grandfather had died and my Dad had disappeared. My Dad was never found. We also saw many foreigners on the beach with lots of wounds, I felt very sorry for them. I want to thank all the people who sent money to help the Tsunami victims."

*The bizarre spectacle of a fishing trawler washed up by the Tsunami next to a house in Khao Lak.* © *Nicholas Mak*

*"The day the Tsunami came, my cousins died. I am very sad about this and I never want the Tsunami to come back again. We don't have much food at home but my Mum sells coffee for a living. Luckily the waves didn't affect my house."*

*Photo: © Nicholas Mak*

*Elephants helping with the clean up after the Tsunami by Nawik.*

"My sister and brother ran for their lives when the Tsunami hit. Luckily they are still alive. I was scared people were going to die. I like school and my ambition is to become a nurse so I can give all I have to the world. When I saw the aftermath of the Tsunami, I was really sad. A lot of my friends died and so did my Dad."

"My name is Kampu and I am 12 years old. I am happy because there are lots of foreigners visiting Khao Lak to help with re-building. I want everybody to see how beautiful Khao Lak used to be and I think it will return to being beautiful again. Already the sea seems clean and blue. Another good thing which has happened since the Tsunami is that we now have volunteer teachers of English from abroad to help us with correct pronunciation. They also teach us lots about other countries and cultures. We hope that the tourists will start coming back to Khao Lak."

*Exhibiting artwork and poetry. © Robin Nagy*

*Previous page: Kampu's drawing shows a happy scene of normality on Khao Lak with two tourists looking out to sea.*

Kampu's poem:

*"Beautiful blue sea.
A sudden catastrophe.
I look back on what happened.
I look back with flowing tears.
Tears which flow back to the sea.
I remember that day in December,
I remember so clearly.
If I could only turn back time,
I'd cry: "don't go to work Mum!
– not by the sea!"*

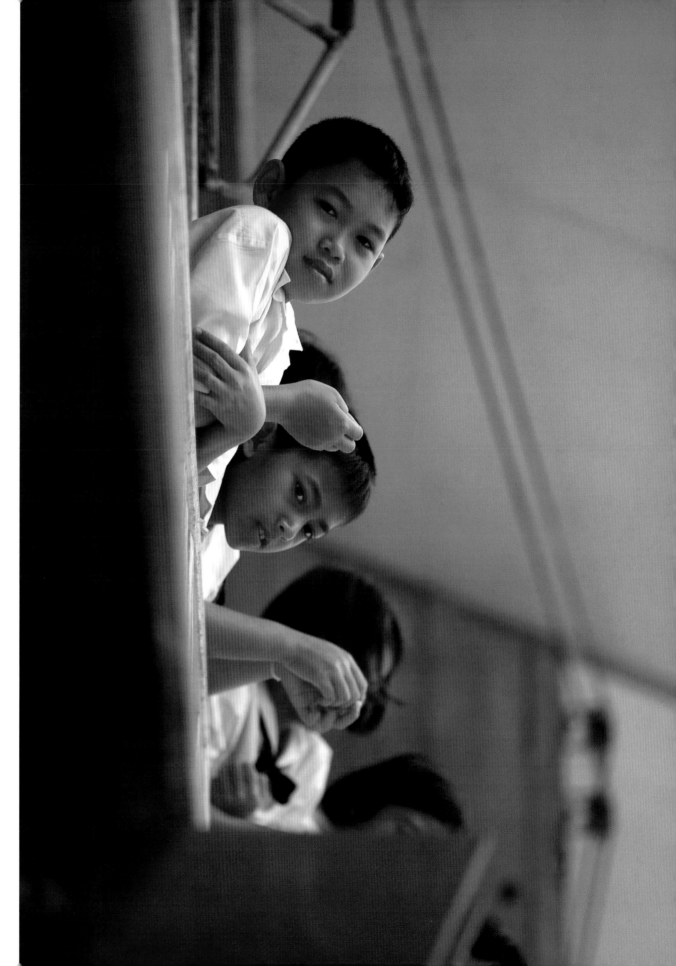

"I am Tom and I am 9 years old. On the day of the Tsunami, I saw it coming. I was so scared that it would come and engulf everything and it did. My friends and family died. My parents were builders. When I grow up I want to be superman so I can help everyone."

*Pak Weep School boys.* © *Nicholas Mak*

"My name is Nawick. When the Tsunami came, my friends told me to come and see all the water. I knew that there was something wrong, because the water was rushing in so quickly. I ran to my Mum and aunt on the beach, who were shouting to tourists and warning them about the wave. When I grow up I want to become a soldier and serve my country like my Dad."

*Drawing by Kamtorn, who also wants to become a soldier, as they played a very important part in the initial aid, clean up and rebuilding efforts at Khao Lak.*

*Drawing by Sut.*

*"My name is Tideran. That day was a Sunday and I was busy playing at home. Whilst I was playing, my uncle told me to run to the car as there was a huge wave coming towards us and we should go to the mountains behind the school. When we arrived on the hill, Dad made us walk up further. We saw the wave rushing in, it was enormous. My family and I stayed there for 3 days before we could go home. Someone said that the wave came and took houses and trees away. Things were scattered everywhere. I now know that the Tsunami was created by an earthquake."*

*A spectacular scene of the Tsunami hitting Khao Lak, drawn by Panrawee.*

"My name is Panwaree, I am 12 years old and in Grade 6 at Bang Niang School. After the Tsunami, I received many presents. I am glad that everyone has been kind and helpful to me. At the moment, I am feeling very happy as people from many different organisations have arranged activities for us. We are very happy, as the school now has many toys that people have kindly donated."

*Bodies strewn on Khao Lak beach by Janjira.*

"My name is Jane and I am 9 years old. My favourite animals are dogs, cats, cows and chickens. I saw the big wave when it came and I was petrified, but not about dying. That day a lot of people did die, which changed my perspective on life. I really appreciate how people came and volunteered to help us and our community."

*A boy bravely rescuing a girl from the Tsunami, as seen by Thippawan.*

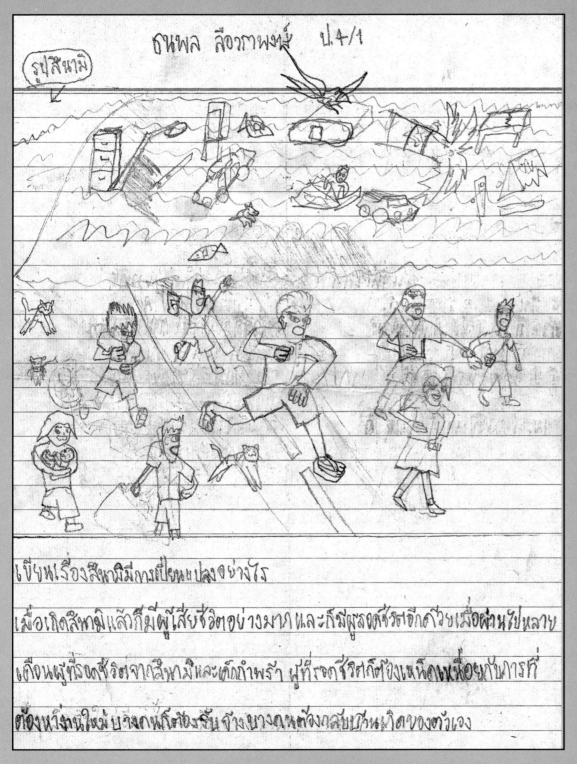

People running away from the Tsunami in Tanaphol's drawing.

"I want to be a soldier when I grow up so that I can help people, like my sister helped me when the Tsunami came. She took me home where we watched as the wave tore everything apart. I was afraid that it would hit my home. Afterwards, I went with my sister to look at what the Tsunami had done and I just wished that everything would go back to the way it was before."

"The Tsunami affected our lives and killed many people. Many months have passed and there are many survivors who are working very hard to find new jobs. Some people have part-time jobs, whilst others are rebuilding their lives in their home towns."

*Supaluk's picture shows everything awash.*

*Girls at Bang Sak School.* © *Robin Nagy*

*"My name is Malinee. On the 26th December at about 9 am in the morning, I was picking mangos with my friends, when we heard the phone ring. My Dad answered and was told that there was a giant wave coming here! My Dad thought they were joking but at about 9.30 am, there was a huge 'BOOM' and lots of people were running around in panic. My Mum and Dad quickly rushed upstairs and I quickly climbed up the mango tree. The big wave washed a lot of people away. Some of my friends lost their loved ones. By now they have accepted the fact that their parents are gone forever. I feel very sorry for them."*

*Drawing by Malinee.*

"My name is Chadatorn and I am 11 years old. After the Tsunami came, I was told that all my family members had died, so I was really depressed. Later on, I learned the good news that some members had survived. I talked to the monk and I was comforted and strengthened. I know that I can keep on going with my life."

*Girl at Pak Weep School. © Nicholas Mak*

*The sun rising on Khao Lak beach, as drawn by Pasit.*

*Suwanna's picture displayed at Bang Niang School.*

*"I didn't personally see the Tsunami, as I was safe at home. The Tsunami made me want to become a doctor so that I can treat my parents when they are in need. I would have been much happier if the waves hadn't struck, as my parents are vendors and can't sell so much now. I love school and learning and I like dogs and fish."*

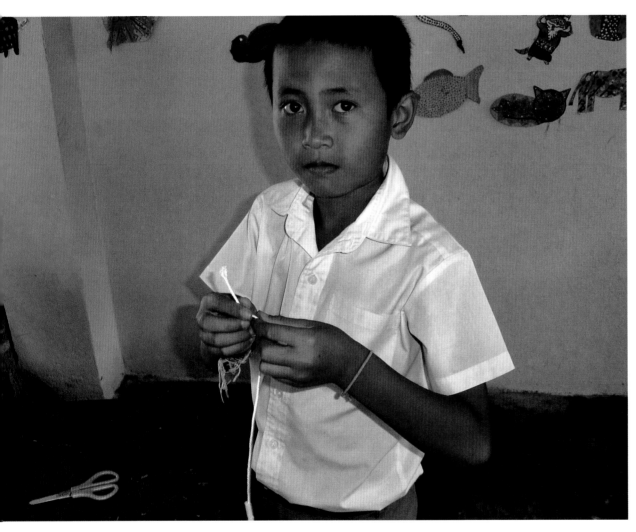

Pak Weep School boy. © Robin Nagy

"26th December. A sunny day.
Running quickly
10.00 am – Death caught up
and came crashing into our
community.
She was very scary.
'Run run, find your loved ones!'
Life beat death. We're glad."

"I ran as fast as I could from the Tsunami. I ran up the hill with everyone else to be safe. Nothing was left of my house, so now I live in a tent. When I grow up, I want to be a nurse so that I can take care of people."

*Daina holding her drawing.*
*© Macha Cauchois*

*Drawing by Daina.*

This photo montage, taken from seven video frame captures (spread over a few seconds), shows people standing on the beach moments before the Tsunami hit the coastline of Khao Lak. The people can be clearly seen on the golden sand of the beach in the top right, as well as on the sea-bed where the sea had 'gone out' twenty minutes before. The photo collage gives a unique impression of the terrifying magnitude of the wave.

*Photo compilation of the Khao Lak Tsunami. © Robin Nagy*

"On Sunday 26th December, a terrible thing happened. I went to the seaside with my friends and we went for a dip in the sea. After a while, the tide suddenly went out, leaving all the fishes flapping around on the wet sand. People went rushing on to the beach to catch the fish. The next thing we knew, a huge wave was racing toward us. I thought the wave was going to crash into the beach, so my friend and I quickly drove our bikes back home. Minutes later, cars were rushing away from the seaside."

Drawing by Meen.

*In the playground at Bang Niang School.* © *Robin Nagy*

**Children of the Tsunami**
*Khao Lak – A Story of Hope*

"My name is Phupay and I am 10 years old. When I saw the Tsunami my Dad, brother and I ran up the mountain. I saw the 813 boat (a police boat) being washed up on the shore. I lost my mother in the Tsunami, as well as belongings like my truck, television and air conditioning. The volunteers are here to support us and give us help. When I grow up, I want to be a doctor so that I can help my Dad, as well as anyone else who is sick. I like school and enjoy reading and drawing."

*Drawing on display at Bang Niang School.*

"The Tsunami snatched away the lives of many people living along the coastal regions of Phuket. I am lucky to be one of the survivors of the catastrophic wave. I was saved because I was collecting sweet vegetables in the forest with my grandmother and brother when the wave struck. I heard a loud whooshing sound, like a plough with a buffalo, rushing past me. I was terrified when I saw that the water was quickly coming towards us. There were trees and coconuts floating everywhere in the water. We managed to out run the onslaught of water that was coming fast and reached the mountain behind the school. I was exhausted and all we had to drink, at that time, was water from the khlong (canal). Later, I walked to my cousin's house to find some food for my family and me. On the way, I looked down the mountain and saw that our houses were now planks of wood drifting in the murky water. We stayed up on the hill for some days before finally returning back down to the Pak Weep School, where the teachers helped care for the survivors."

*Drawing by June.*

"My name is Paina. The day of the Tsunami, we were at my mother's friend's house. He mentioned the odd level of the water, noting the tide seemed to have gone out a long way. He borrowed my mother's car to go and pick up his children who were at the beach. When he was half way there, he saw the destructive wave hit. My mother's friend drove as quickly as he could and when he finally arrived home, he fainted. He had lost his beloved wife and children. Please remember all the innocent lives that were lost in the Tsunami."

*A drawing on display at Bang Niang School.*

*Drawing by Jaroenwai in Year 1 showing two tsunamis.*

*Making paper snakes at Pak Weep School. © Robin Nagy*

*Pak Weep children. © Robin Nagy*

*Natcha's drawing shows the sea 'going out' before the Tsunami came in.*

"I'm Chir and I'm 10 years old. On the day of the Tsunami I was at home. My uncle suddenly said, "there's no water in the sea!" Then he gave his motorcycle to my other uncle, my father's younger brother, and told us to go up the mountain, while he stayed to lock up the house. That was the last time I saw my uncle. I am very sorry that he was never found."

"My name is Banrawit and I am 11 years old. On the 26th of December I was very scared. I ran to the mountains and whilst I was running, my heart was beating really fast. From the mountains I could clearly see the Tsunami. I was afraid my home would be destroyed, but fortunately the wave didn't reach it. I ran back home and stayed there as the alarm for the second Tsunami sounded. I didn't want to leave my house, because I was scared people would steal our possessions."

*Ying's story about nature and how peaceful life was before the Tsunami with her friends.*

"My name is Rungthong. I am very happy that so many volunteers have come to help those affected by the Tsunami. Not only have they helped the people themselves, but they have also helped with rebuilding the houses and the schools. The school I go to was affected by the Tsunami and many foreigners have come to help. They have brought with them toys and essential items as well as stationary. I am very happy that these people have come to help and to carry out various activities at my school as well as at many other schools that were affected by the Tsunami."

*Drawing and story by Rungthong.*

สึกนามิ

ฉันดีใจมากที่มีคนช่วยเหลือผู้คนที่ถูกสึกนามิและยังช่วย เหลือบ้านเรือนและโรงเรียนโรงเรียนที่ฉันอยู่เป็นโรงเรียน ที่ถูกสึกนามิและมีคนต่างประเทศมาช่วยเหลือ นำของเล่น ของใช้ และเครื่องเรียนเครื่องเขียนฉันดีใจมากที่มีคนมาใช้ เลือกโรงเรียนและมีคนมาทำกิจกรรมทำโรงเรียนและ ยังได้ไปทำกิจกรรมที่โรงเรียนอื่นๆอีกหลายโรงเรียน

ด.ญ รุ่งทอง ทองคำกัลยา

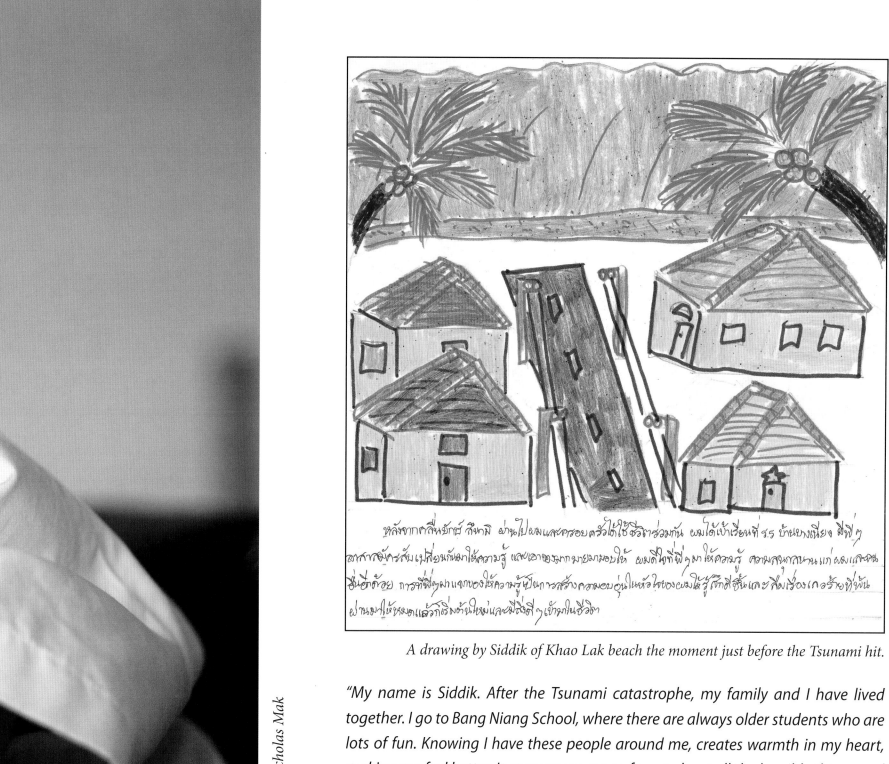

*Photo: © Nicholas Mak*

หลังจากคลื่นยักษ์ สึนามิ ผ่านไปผมและครอบครัวได้ใช้ชีวิตร่วมกัน ผมได้เข้าเรียนที่ ร.ร. บ้านบางเนียง มีพี่ๆ อาภารอังคารสับเปลี่ยนกันมาให้ความรู้ และเอาขนมมากมายมามอบให้ ผมดีใจที่พี่ๆมาให้ความรู้ ความสุกกสนานแก่ ผมและเพื่อน อันอีกด้วย การที่พี่ๆมาแจกของให้ความรู้เป็นการสร้างความอบอุ่นในหัวใจของผมให้รู้สึกดีขึ้นและลืมเรื่องเกวร้ายที่ผัน ผ่านมาให้หมดแล้วก็เริ่มต้นบ้านใหม่และมีสิ่งดีๆ เข้ามาในชีวิต

*A drawing by Siddik of Khao Lak beach the moment just before the Tsunami hit.*

"My name is Siddik. After the Tsunami catastrophe, my family and I have lived together. I go to Bang Niang School, where there are always older students who are lots of fun. Knowing I have these people around me, creates warmth in my heart, making me feel better. It encourages me to forget about all the horrible things and helps me move on to a fresh new start, filled with hope."

*Drawing by Chadatorn.*

*Friendship around the world drawn by Christel.*

*Joey's drawing shows a rescue helicopter at work.*

*Drawing by Wilawan.*

*The aftermath of the Tsunami.*

*Drawing by Sritaa.*

*Drawing by Pachanida.*

*An evocative black tsunami.*

"My name is Joni and I am 14 years old. When the Tsunami came, I ran away with my brother and sister. I was very scared that people would die. When I saw what it had done I was so sad. More than 10 of my friends died as well as my father."

*Classes lining up at Bang Sak School ready to go home.*

"On the morning of the Tsunami I was watching 'Gomint' on the TV at my friend's house. I saw the wave rushing to the shore. My sister and mother ran up the hill and I ran home with my Dad. We were all very lucky."

Photo: © Robin Nagy

*"Even if we saw our parents die in the Tsunami, we must not feel like there is no point living, but remember that there are still many people who care for us. There are lots of people who visit us and support us and play with us. It makes us happy and we remember to enjoy every day. I want my friends, whose parents lost their lives, not to worry or be sad. I think that their parents are not suffering and have gone to heaven."*

*What's left of a house after the Tsunami.*
*© Robin Nagy*

"My name is Balinya. My Mum was at work at a hotel when the big wave came. I ran away with my Dad. Later I found out that my Mum and aunt had been washed away by the waves. I miss my Mum and sometimes I cry. My Dad works at the hotel now. When I grow up, I want to be a policeman."

Why is it that euphemisms are used to describe harsh truths? Is it in order that people like me can feel less guilty about failing to appreciate what we've got?

We left Khao Lak knowing that life can be harsh and unfair, some of us already knew this (in varying degrees) from personal experience, yet our vicarious encounter with the Tsunami seemed to give the rather clichéd maxim 'life's unfair' new meaning. And yet the process of recovery was already well underway. Through the effort of many aid agencies, volunteers, the Thai Army and local people, new houses have already been built and many families have already moved into their new

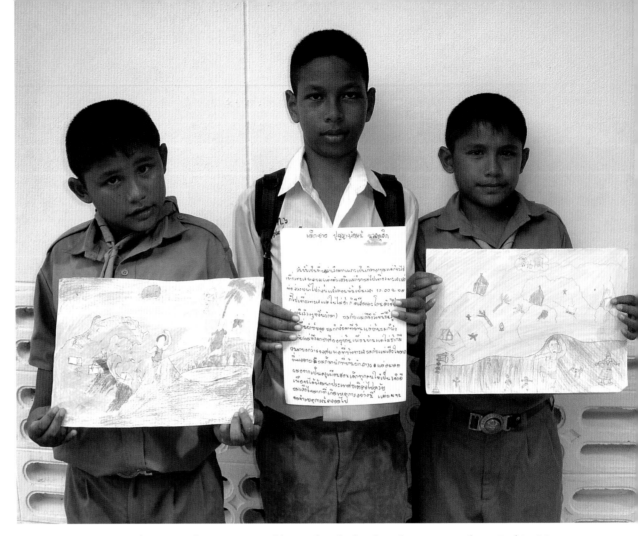

*Boys from Watkommaneeyakhet School display their artwork. © Robin Nagy*

homes. As the saying goes, "behind every cloud there is a silver lining". The children we visited were solid silver. Their limitless energy and enthusiasm reminded us that all's not lost. They will grow up and will in turn help to ensure that Khao Lak recovers from this appalling disaster.

Each of us came to Khao Lak with different agendas. Some might say we had a perhaps arrogant, even patronising wish to 'help these children'. But, instead, of us helping them, they helped us. They helped us see that things which appear so normal and permanent to us are transitory and can all be washed away within a few minutes. They showed that even when everything you have ever had, loved and worked for, has been taken from you, what remains is hope; and this book is their story of hope.

# ACKNOWLEDGEMENTS

We would like to thank the following sponsors for supporting our project so generously. Without their financial donations we would not have been able to produce the book.

**Mr and Mrs P. Kirketerp**

PRO Services

 ITT Industries

**Mr R. Siew**

**The Lancaster Family**

**Ipedex (Thailand) Ltd.**

**PREMIER OILFIELD SERVICES CO., LTD**

We would also like to thank those sponsors who have preferred to remain anonymous and all those who have helped support the project in other ways, in particular Philip Adkins, Abigail Barnett, Richard Campbell, Ajarn Sompoch Chaipadungnirand (Bang Niang School), Kaewta Chaisavas, Pornpimol Charoen, Emma Davies, M. L. Pariyada Diskul, Sally Flint, Andrew Gordon, Nick Hazell, Isobel Hedges, Isabella Henderson, Jackie Houghton, Sharon Jones, Jan Lyde, Nicholas Mak, Sara Martin, Ajarn Watana Mitwong (Pakweek School), Anita Pardoe, Ajarn Prasith Sathapornjaturavith (Bang Sak School), Kirsten Simmons, Darren Taylor, Robert Thornhill, Ajarn Suchart Wangviseth (Watkommaneeyakhet School) and Pirayos Wongthongsuk. Your belief in the project is what has made it succeed. Thank you also to Frances Nagy who came up with the original idea for the book.

# PROJECT TEAM

**Students :**

Macha Cauchois
Nachanok Visitsak
Bo Ling Leung
Janna De Vos
Derrick Lee
Felicity Lyde
Suthirat Owlarn
Christel Ridao
Nicholas Siew
Oliver Adkins
Vinushini Arunagiri
Ambrish Bandalkul
Alvin Chen
Chih Yen Chen
Dora Cheung
Willem D Coetzee
Bethany Dent
Tarin Doty
Namnuang Eamcharoenying
Ritika Gandhi
Ashleigh Gray
Nicole Hardman
Callum Henderson
Nishant Jayadev
Neha Kant
Jesper Kirketerp
Christopher Klocke
Rachel Kwok
Ludivine Lacrosse
Adam Longden
Nicholas Mak
Dawn Mekunwattana
Michael Nardone

Regina Ng
Andrea Noble
Erica Ong
Momo Onishi
Emily Parsons
Natasha Saito
Punthita Sakuntanaga
Jasper Sng
Kushagra Sodhia
Virada Suphantarida
Natthanich Surawuthipong
Nadeenut Suvanprakorn
Suferne Tam
Nalin Tejavibulya
Priya Thakral
Jong Shuh Tsay
Geraldine Uba
Warakorn Watanachowapisut
Methawe Wattanasarnvechakul

**Teachers and Contributors:**

Robin Nagy
Jackie Houghton
Pornpimol Charoen
Kirsten Simmons
Sally Flint
Emma Davies
Richard Campbell
Sara Martin
Sharon Jones